Unicorn Toddler Coloring Book

Simple Coloring
for Ages 1-3

Published in 2017 by
Nyx Spectrum

ISBN: 978 0 9988447 1 8

Printed in the United States of America

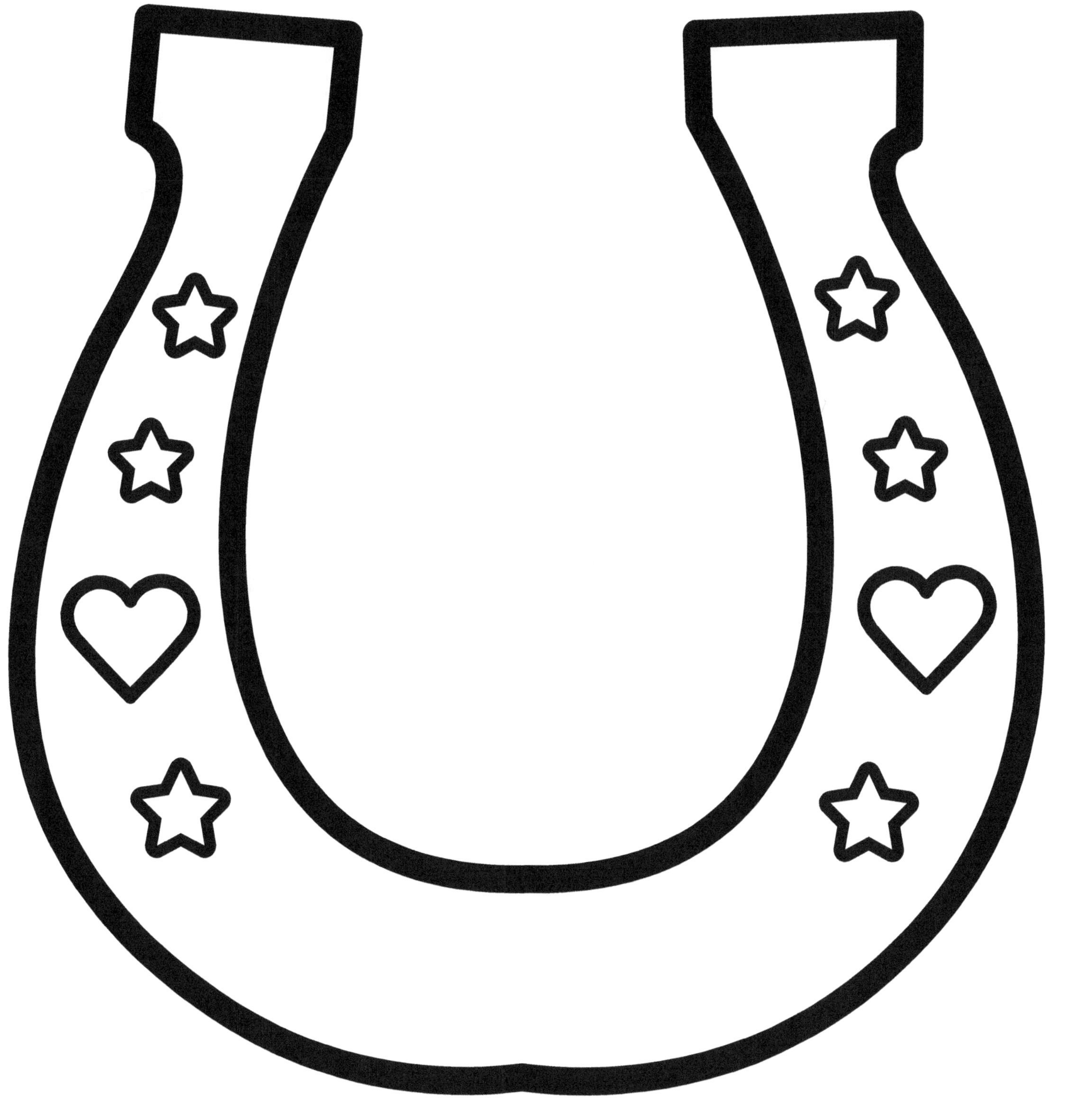

www.ingramcontent.com/pod-product-compliance
Lightning Source LLC
Chambersburg PA
CBHW081257040426
42452CB00014B/2544
* 9 7 8 0 9 9 8 8 4 4 7 1 8 *